S0-BEP-030

The General Store

by Rennay Craats

WEIGL EDUCATIONAL PUBLISHERS

Published by Weigl Educational Publishers Limited
6325-10 Street SE
Calgary, Alberta
Canada T2H 2Z9
Web site: www.weigl.com

Canadian Cataloguing in Publication Data
Craats, Rennay, 1973-
    The general store / Rennay Craats.

(Early Canadian life)
Includes index.
ISBN 1-55388-039-0 (lib. bound: alk. paper)
ISBN 1-55388-055-2 (pbk.)

    1. General stores--Canada--History--Juvenile literature. 2. Frontier and pioneer life--Canada--Juvenile literature.
I. Title. II. Series: Early Canadian life (Calgary, Alta.)

HF5429.6.C3C73 2003   j381'.14'0971   C2003-905432-2

Printed and bound in the United States of America
1 2 3 4 5 6 7 8 9 0   06 05 04 03

We acknowledge the financial support of the Government of Canada through the Book Publishing Industry Development Program (BPIDP) for our publishing activities.

Photograph Credits

Archives of Ontario (Bartle Brothers/10002513): pages 1, 6; **Ellen Bryan**: pages 3T, 10; **Canada Science and Technology Museum**: page 14T; **Comstock, Inc.**: page 19; **Corbis Corporation**: page 20; **Karen Crawford/Daystar Images**: page 23R; **Glenbow Archives**: pages 8 (NC-60-76), 11 (NA-3626-1), 15M (NA-2717-3), 15B (NA-849-12), 16 (NC-43-12); **Nova Scotia Museum**: page 18 (P270.123); **photocanada.com**: pages 5, 14B, 15T; **Photos.com**: pages 3B, 13T, 13B; **Saskatchewan Archives Board**: page 7; **Tina Schwartzenberger**: pages 4, 9, 12, 23L.

Project Coordinator
Tina Schwartzenberger

Design
Janine Vangool

Layout
Bryan Pezzi

Copy Editor
Wendy Cosh

Photo Researchers
Ellen Bryan
Barbara Hoffman

Contents

Introduction

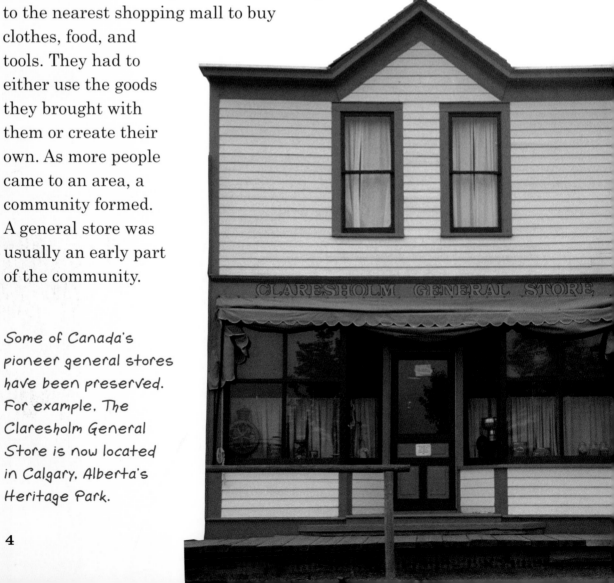

Canada's early settlers often left their homes with few belongings. The first settlers came to a land of wilderness. They had to create their own farms. The pioneers could not go to the nearest shopping mall to buy clothes, food, and tools. They had to either use the goods they brought with them or create their own. As more people came to an area, a community formed. A general store was usually an early part of the community.

Some of Canada's pioneer general stores have been preserved. For example, The Claresholm General Store is now located in Calgary, Alberta's Heritage Park.

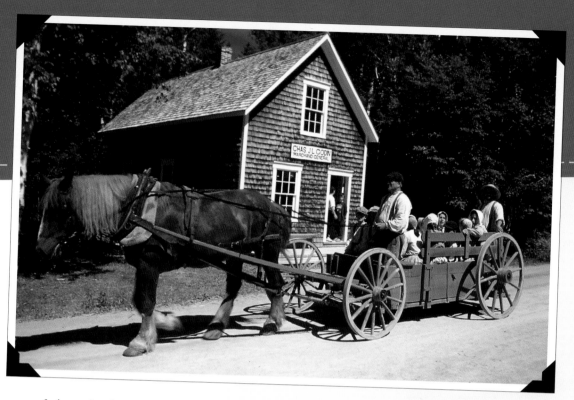

A trip to town to visit the general store was a welcome relief from the hard work of daily farm life.

Canadian pioneers relied on the general store for everything from food to shoes. These stores became the centres of early Canadian towns. For many people, a trip to the general store took the whole day. For some, it was an overnight **excursion**. Pioneer families often looked forward to "going to town." There, they could catch up on the latest news and visit friends. They also stocked up on the goods they needed for the weeks ahead.

Did you know:

Shopkeepers were a valuable source of information, both **gossip** and facts. Townspeople and travellers gathered at general stores to visit as well as to purchase goods.

Tents, Logs, and False Fronts

Early general stores were sometimes just tents and packing crates. As communities became more settled, shopkeepers built permanent buildings for their goods. Most general stores started out as small log buildings. As business got better, owners made the stores larger. Stores—especially in western Canada—often had false fronts with the owner's name in large letters along the top.

False fronts on general stores were popular in Canada from 1849 to 1898.

Hudson's Bay Company stores were created so that settlers and Canada's Native Peoples could trade goods with each other.

Many of Canada's first general stores were associated with the Hudson's Bay Company. These stores could not meet the needs of growing settlements. Families across the country began to open their own shops. Most stores were built along railroad lines so that they could serve more customers.

Did you know:

Canada's first stores were trading posts that did business mostly with Canada's Native Peoples. Trading posts were built close to rivers and lakes to make transporting goods easier.

First-hand account:

Canada's early general stores were very different from the stores we shop at today. Here is one pioneer's memories of general stores.

The old general stores would be described as dark and dismal and perhaps not even clean by today's standards. Many of the buildings housing these stores were two-storey with living quarters for the owners or renters, upstairs. Some had living quarters in the back.

The Shopkeepers

Most general stores were family businesses. As the family grew, so could the business. Even with several family members helping, running a general store required hard work. Families worked from dawn to dusk to stay in business. Shopkeepers knew that the community depended on them to **import** supplies that were needed throughout the year. These supplies included coffee, fabric, flour, and sugar.

The general store owner and shopkeeper knew everyone in the community as they all visited the store.

Did you know:

Many general store shopkeepers gave farmers credit for up to one year. Farmers were often unable to pay their bills until they had harvested their crops.

Shelves behind the counter in the general store displayed canned goods and other items for sale.

Canadian shopkeepers had many responsibilities. They were accountants, bankers, merchants, and shelf stockers. They worked long hours and did not make much money. Shopkeepers ran their shops because they loved the people in their communities. Shopkeepers' generosity and kindness kept many families from going hungry when families found themselves unable to pay their bills.

First-hand account:

A Fort Langley, B.C. shopkeeper remembers his best-selling items in 1858.

Articles in demand were blankets and woolen clothing, tinware such as pots and frying pans, various mining tools including pans and pickaxes, and provisions, principally flour, bacon, beans and molasses.

Flour and Fabric

Canadian pioneers bought clothing, farming equipment, fresh meat, and other groceries at the general store. The store was more than just a place to purchase goods. The store was also the **hub** of the pioneer community. People visited with one another at the general store. The post office was often located in the town's general store. People dropped off letters and packages for family in other parts of Canada.

As a community grew larger, the general store offered a wider variety of goods for sale.

By 1900, some general stores housed the town's telegraph equipment. A telegraph sends messages over long distances by sending electronic pulses through a wire.

The general store building could also meet the community's other needs. New towns often did not have schools. The store could be used as a school until one was built. Visitors or newcomers could even sleep in the shop until they found their own homes.

First-hand account:

One early pioneer remembers people leaving parcels for others to pick up at the general store.

(General stores) also were places where packages could be left to be picked up. If a woman wished to send a dress to her daughter who lived some distance away, she sent it to the store to be delivered by the first passer by. Often stores took on the appearance of baggage rooms.

Tools of the Shopkeeper

Pioneer shopkeepers used many tools every day. Their tools were different from those used in stores today. Pioneer shopkeepers did not have scanners to tell them the price of an item or computers that added up the customer's purchase. Their tools were simple.

Cash Boxes

Canadian pioneer shopkeepers used wooden boxes, and later, metal cabinets, to hold their cash. The cabinets had drawers for coins and bills. The cabinets were eventually replaced with cash registers. Buttons on the cash registers showed dollar amounts. The register gave the shopkeeper the total amount the customer owed. These cash registers slowly **evolved** into the computer systems used in many stores today.

Account Books

Shopkeepers kept **ledger** books. Each customer had an account at the store. The customer's account was kept in the ledger book. The shopkeepers checked the books often to make sure a customer did not owe too much money. Shopkeepers also used ledger books to keep track of sales and **inventory**.

Scales

Many products, such as flour and spices, were bought in bulk and sold by weight. Shopkeepers could estimate the desired weight of a product using their hands. Scales allowed the shopkeeper to give the customer the exact amount of a product that they wanted. Different scales were used to weigh mail, food, and hardware products like nails.

A Day in the Life

Most shopkeepers and their families lived above or behind their store. A typical day for a Canadian pioneer shopkeeper may have been like this.

7:00 a.m.

Shopkeepers started working early in the morning. Once the doors opened, the entire family was put to work. One of the first jobs for many shopkeepers was to drop the mail off at the train station. After railway routes were in place, mail schedules were created. Shopkeepers rushed to drop off bags of letters and packages for the mail train in the morning.

8:00 a.m.

By 8:00 am, the male shopkeeper was cutting and stacking wood at the back of the store. He cut wood for the fire in his store and to sell to customers throughout the year. The female shopkeeper often spent the entire day working behind the counter. Her first job on cold days was to start the fire in the stove. She kept the fire burning all day. If there were no customers waiting when she first opened the store, the female shopkeeper would stock and tidy the shelves.

noon

The male and female shopkeepers ate lunch separately because someone always needed to be working in the store. After lunch, the male shopkeeper delivered goods to customers who could not haul them on their own. The female shopkeeper continued to weigh goods for sale, accept items for credit, enter credit items in the ledger book, and clean up small spills.

4:00 p.m.

The shopkeeper's children returned from school around 4:00 pm. The children swept the floors and dusted the shelves and counters. They also restocked the shelves with merchandise. Children could be counted on to help package such goods as dates, rolled oats, and sugar by weight. The male shopkeeper often rushed to meet the incoming mail train late in the afternoon. He picked up letters and parcels and took them back to the store.

6:00 p.m.

The family did not eat their supper together because someone had to stay in the store and help customers. Some days there was more time for supper because there were few customers. Often, however, supper was eaten quickly, and everyone went right back to work.

Cash, Credit, or Crop?

Canadian pioneers tried to raise or grow most of their food. Families needed to purchase some items such as coffee and shoes that they could not grow or make themselves. Customers traded with shopkeepers for those items. This is called the **barter** system. Farmers **churned** extra butter and gathered extra eggs for bartering.

Butter and eggs were commonly traded for sugar and flour at the general store.

Bartering challenged shopkeepers. It took time to decide an item's value. Shopkeepers had to find a place to store the items until they could use or sell them. Sometimes the trade was not fair. The customer may have brought extra chickens or grain beyond what was owed. The shopkeeper kept the extra items and credited the customer's account. The next time that customer was in the store, the credit went toward their purchase. Most shopkeepers welcomed the business, even if bartering was not easy.

First-hand account:

One Ontario shopkeeper shares his memories of the barter system. A few unusual payments stand out in his mind.

In those years, I took thirty-two cows 'on account,' rented them out to farmers and sold them a few years later when prices were better. I also took twelve horses and colts 'on account,' as well as pigs and turkeys. Very little money changed hands, you traded in things; whatever you could get, you took.

Gathering at the General Store

Pioneers often gathered at general stores. Men sat around the store on upturned crates, benches, and kegs. Some leaned against the counter and talked about current events. Before long, someone brought out the checkerboard, and customers sat down to a game. The stove was the heart of the store. On cold days, people stopped by the stove to warm up. The stove was a place to **congregate**, tell stories, and visit with neighbours.

John and Samuel Cumminger owned the Cumminger Brothers General Store in Sherbrooke, Nova Scotia. They, like other store owners, were important members of their community.

Christmas trees were one way to add Christmas cheer to the general store.

First-hand account:

One Canadian pioneer remembers how much her grandfather enjoyed visiting the general store.

Grandpa, when he was not on the boats, went every night to the store in Harwood. So the men did the shopping. Mother, I don't think she was in that store half a dozen times. Grandpa would go there and sit and visit, and then he would come home with the stories...

Did you know:

Letters from far-away loved ones caused a great deal of excitement. When the shopkeeper brought the heavy mail bag to the store, everyone gathered to see who would get mail.

Christmas was a special time at the general store. Many customers visited the store. Shopkeepers sold special items to give as gifts. Special ingredients needed for baking and holiday dinners were stocked, too. The general store was also a place where townspeople could gather to wish each other "Merry Christmas!" Many shopkeepers hung special holiday decorations. The store was a festive and cheery place to be during the holiday season.

General Stores Past and Present

As the years passed and towns grew, many general stores could no longer stay in business. Large companies opened stores that provided goods for lower prices. Some stores specialized in certain items, such as tools. Today, very few general stores still exist. Canadians are more likely to visit grocery stores and shopping malls to buy food, clothing, and tools.

Inventory

Which of the items listed below would you find in pioneer general stores and grocery stores today? Which items would you find only in an early Canadian general store?

candy	flour
clothing	mail
coffee	nails
eggs	shoes
farming equipment	wood

Most families today go to grocery stores to buy food. They do not barter, but they often shop as a family.

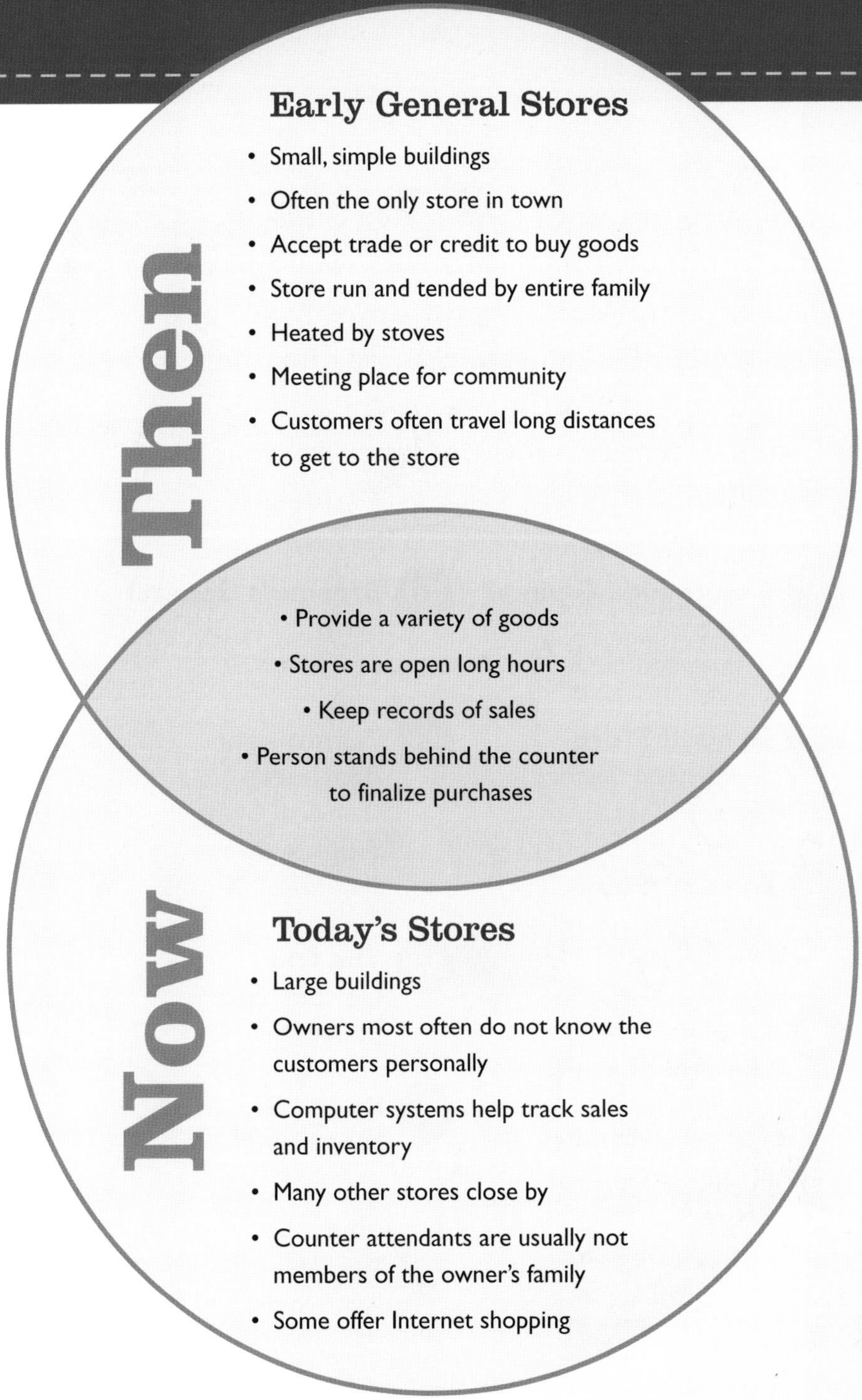

Then

Early General Stores

- Small, simple buildings
- Often the only store in town
- Accept trade or credit to buy goods
- Store run and tended by entire family
- Heated by stoves
- Meeting place for community
- Customers often travel long distances to get to the store

- Provide a variety of goods
- Stores are open long hours
- Keep records of sales
- Person stands behind the counter to finalize purchases

Now

Today's Stores

- Large buildings
- Owners most often do not know the customers personally
- Computer systems help track sales and inventory
- Many other stores close by
- Counter attendants are usually not members of the owner's family
- Some offer Internet shopping

DIAGRAM

There are many differences between pioneer general stores and stores operating today. There are some similarities between the two as well. The diagram on the left compares these similarities and differences. Copy the diagram in your notebook. Try to think of other similarities and differences to add to your diagram.

As you can see by the diagram, stores today have some things in common with general stores 100 years ago.

Preserving the Past

oday, many historic societies work to preserve general stores. They recreate what the general stores would have looked like in pioneer days. Some general stores have been turned into pioneer museums to remember early Canadian life. Others have maintained an **authentic** look on the outside but are modern stores inside. Here are a few Canadian general stores that operate as museums, historical sites, and stores.

1 **Kilby Historic Store and Farm**
Harrison Mills, BC

2 **H. Kershaw & Son General Store and Post Office**
Fort Steele Heritage Town, Fort Steele, BC

3 **Claresholm General Store**
Heritage Park Historical Village, Calgary, AB

4 **General Store on Boomtown Street**
Western Development Museum, Saskatoon, SK

5 **Commanda General Store**
Commanda, ON

6 **General Store**
Southwestern Ontario Heritage Village, Essex, ON

7 **General Store**
Westfield Heritage Village, Hamilton, ON

8 **Le Brun General Store**
Trois-Rivières, QB

9 **Hodges General Store**
Missisquoi Museum, Stanbridge East, QB

10 **Barbour's General Store**
Saint John, NB

11 **Cumminger Brothers General Store**
Sherbrooke Village, Sherbrooke, NS

12 **The Old General Store**
Murray River, PEI

13 **Kean's General Store**
Brookfield, NL

Claresholm
General Store

H. Kershaw & Son General
Store and Post Office

Glossary

Authentic: real; genuine and true

Barter: exchange goods for other goods

Churned: beat milk to make butter

Congregate: gather together

Evolved: to gradually develop over time

Excursion: an outing or journey to a place and back

Gossip: talk about other people's lives and business

Hub: central point of activity

Import: to bring in goods from another country for sale or use

Inventory: a detailed list of goods and their value

Ledger: a book used to record money transactions

Index